Boxer

Boxer

Border Collie

Boxer

Chihuahua

Yorkshire Terrier

Yorkshire Terrier

Australian Shepherd

Yorkshire Terrier

Australian Shepherd

Chihuahua

Australian Shepherd

Bernese Mountain Dog

Bernese Mountain Dog

Beagle

Bernese Mountain Dog

Cardigan Welsh Corgi

Cardigan Welsh Corgi

French Bulldog

French Bulldog

French Bulldog

German Shepherd

Dachshund

Labrador Retriever

German Shepherd

German Shepherd

Dachshund

Dachshund

Mixed Breed

Mixed Breed

Dachshund

Greyhound

Greyhound

Labrador Retriever

Labrador Retriever

Pug

Pug

Labrador Retriever

Pug

Labrador Retriever

Miniature Schnauzer

Labrador Retriever

Siberian Husky

Siberian Husky

Golden Retriever

Siberian Husky

TO APPLY A
TATTOO

1 Cut out the tattoo and remove the plastic cover.

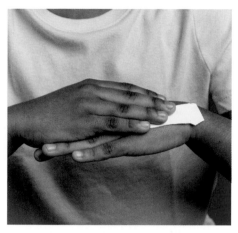

2 Stick the tattoo, picture-side down, onto clean, dry skin.

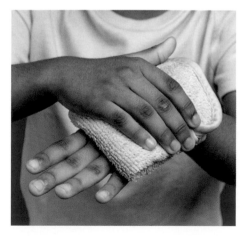

3 Place a wet cloth over the tattoo. Press down gently for about 30 seconds. Hold it still!

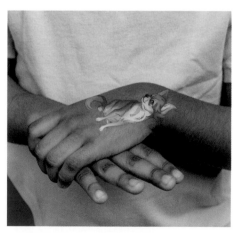

4 Gently slide off the paper backing. Do not touch until it's dry.

TIP: To remove tattoos, dab with rubbing alcohol or baby oil. Wait 10 seconds, then rub gently. Apply more rubbing alcohol or baby oil repeatedly until removed.

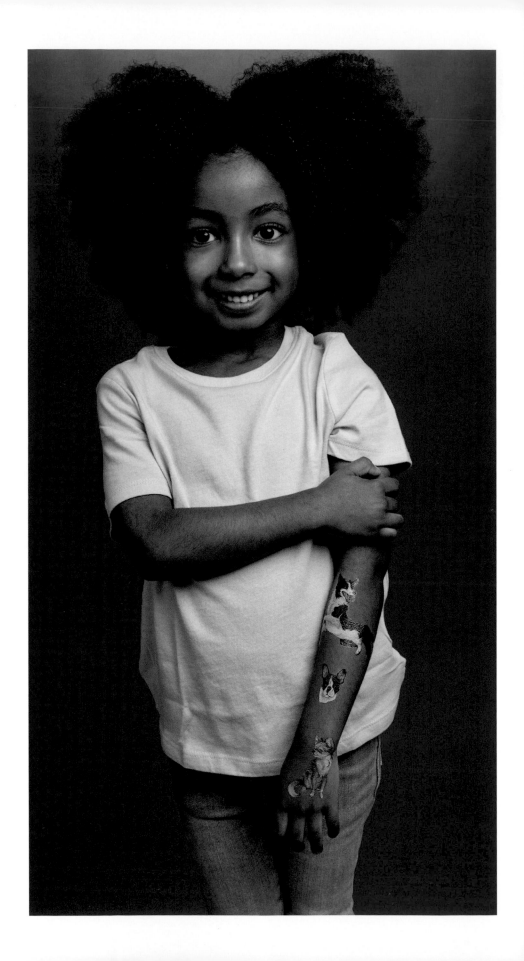

◄ AUSTRALIAN SHEPHERD

Despite its name, the Australian shepherd is an American breed. These active, intelligent dogs are superb herders who are often used to work cattle.

BEAGLE ►

An excellent hunting dog, the beagle is also a cheerful, affectionate, and playful family companion.

With their outstanding noses, beagles can be trained to sniff out problems in hotels like mold and bedbugs!

BERNESE MOUNTAIN DOG ►

These dogs are as sweet-natured and loving as they are beautiful. Their long, silky coats are always tricolor: black, white, and rust.

BORDER COLLIE ▼

Energetic and intelligent, border collies like to have a job. Bred to herd sheep, they need plenty of exercise. Black and white is the most common color combination but they also come in many other colors.

Border collies excel in many sporting events, such as disc dog competitions.

BOXER ➤

Bred centuries ago as hunting dogs, boxers are excellent watchdogs and have served as police and military dogs. They are loyal and affectionate with their families.

◄ CHIHUAHUA

These tiny dogs love to snuggle but are always happy to romp and play. They can be smooth coated or longhaired and weigh less than 6 pounds.

The Chihuahua is the national dog of Mexico.

DACHSHUND ∨

Bred in Germany to hunt badgers, dachshunds are smart, strong, and brave. With a big bark, they are good watchdogs and loyal family members.

Dachshunds can be smooth coated, wirehaired, or longhaired.

FRENCH BULLDOG ➤

One of the most popular breeds in the world, the Frenchie, as it's called, is easily recognized by its big "bat" ears, flat nose, and charming personality.

With their short noses, Frenchies are prone to overheating and snoring. They are not very good swimmers.

◄ GERMAN SHEPHERD

Originally bred to herd sheep, the multitalented German shepherd is a faithful and affectionate family companion who shines at any activity that calls for strength, agility, and intelligence.

German shepherds were used during World War I to carry messages and ammunition, and also to help search for missing or injured soldiers.

GOLDEN RETRIEVER ▾

The golden retriever's gorgeous coat matches this breed's sunny temperament and friendly nature. These smart, athletic dogs make wonderful family pets and excellent service dogs.

Most goldens love to swim and chase after balls.

GREYHOUND ▾

These lean, long-legged sight hounds are descended from dogs bred to chase prey in the deserts of Egypt thousands of years ago. They love to run but are also happy to curl up on a couch.

The greyhound, the fastest of all dogs, is able to sprint up to 45 miles an hour for short distances.

◄ LABRADOR RETRIEVER

The high-energy Lab is one of America's most popular breeds, beloved for its friendly, outgoing personality, eagerness to please, and versatility as a service dog and family pet.

Black, chocolate, and yellow puppies may all be part of a single litter of Labs.

MINIATURE SCHNAUZER ➤

These friendly, active dogs love to be with their families, whether going for a hike or lounging at home. Their distinctive bushy eyebrows and full beards require regular grooming.

There are two larger types of schnauzers: standard and giant.

MIXED-BREED DOGS ∨

Mixed-breed dogs, sometimes called mutts, have parents of at least two different breeds, sometimes more. That means they can look like either parent or both, or something totally different. They can have any mix of personality traits, intelligence, and athletic ability, but like most dogs, they all want to be loved!

It's fun to guess what breeds are part of a mutt's heritage.

CARDIGAN WELSH CORGI ⌄

Often described as a big dog in a small body, the corgi is a strong, sturdy dog bred to herd cattle by nipping at their heels. They are surprisingly fast despite their short legs.

The Pembroke Welsh corgi looks similar to the Cardigan, but its tail is cropped short.

POODLE ➤

Beautiful, athletic, and very smart, poodles were originally bred to retrieve waterfowl. Their curly coats protect them from water and cold weather. Poodles come in a variety of colors and three sizes: standard, miniature, and toy.

Poodles must be groomed regularly or have their coats clipped short so the curls don't get tangled.

◀ PUG

One of the oldest breeds, pugs are instantly recognizable, with their flattened faces, round heads, and curly tails. Their friendly, affectionate nature and easy-going attitude make them popular around the world.

SIBERIAN HUSKY ➤

A compact and powerful dog with boundless energy, the Siberian husky loves to be part of a family. Teams of them can travel for miles over frozen ground pulling loaded sleds.

Siberian huskies can have blue or brown eyes. Some dogs have one of each color!

◀ YORKSHIRE TERRIER

Though now thought of as pampered lapdogs, Yorkies are true terriers, bred in England to hunt rats in mines and mills. They are friendly, alert, and very affectionate with the people they love.